OGDEN NASH:
Playing with Words

by Jiang Qingling
illustrated by Franklin Hammond

HOUGHTON MIFFLIN BOSTON

hippopotamus

octopus

orange

Can you think of a word that rhymes with *hippopotamus?* How about *octopus?* Or *orange?* Do you find it difficult to rhyme these words? Most people do. A clever American poet named Ogden Nash, however, looked at words as though they were puzzle pieces. He took on the challenge of being able to rhyme any word.

Ogden Nash used both real and made-up words throughout his poems. Even when he invented words of his own, however, he saw to it that they made sense in the context of a poem. He loved to play with words in this way, and his rhymes were often funny. For example, in one poem he rhymed *panther* with *anther*, playing on the sound of the word *answer*.

Whether he was working with long words, short words, words with one syllable or many, Nash was able to rhyme any word in—or not in—the dictionary. For this he is remembered as one of America's most beloved poets.

panther

Ogden Nash was born in Rye, New York, on August 19, 1902. He was the fourth of five children, with two sisters, Gwen and Eleanor, and two brothers, Ted and Aubrey.

When Ogden was seven years old, he developed a serious eye infection. As part of his treatment, he had to stay in a dark room for nearly a year. Since he was not allowed to put strain on his eyes, his mother, Mattie, read to him every day. She did not want an illness to stop her son's education. Ogden enthusiastically listened to the lessons that his mother taught. Through this experience, he acquired a passion for learning. He also developed a sharp memory, an active imagination, and a love of language.

Ogden's mother was one of many family members, across multiple generations, who understood the value of a good education. In the mid-1800s, Ogden's grandfather (Mattie's father) opened a private school in Kentucky, where he educated his three daughters. When it was time to apply to college, each daughter applied to a male-only college, giving only the initial of her first name. All three daughters were accepted for admission—until the schools discovered that they were women. Once the schools realized what had happened, they reversed their decisions and denied admission to each of the sisters.

As one of those sisters, Mattie felt extremely frustrated. However, she became determined to continue with her schooling. Eventually Mattie attended Wellesley College, an all-female college in Massachusetts.

Mattie Nash wanted to share her love of learning. She hoped that others would be able to appreciate the joy of learning from a young age as she had. Once Mattie had her own children, she helped her sons and daughters learn about topics ranging from languages to history. Her efforts paid off. Mattie was one of the most important teachers in her son Ogden's life.

By the time he was ten, Ogden Nash had learned a great deal about many different subjects. Even more important, his mother's teachings had piqued his interest in writing, and soon Ogden was inventing his own stories. His enthusiasm, creativity, imagination, and sense of humor contributed to everything he wrote.

Ogden wrote funny rhymes. He wrote poems about animals around him and about common life experiences. His grandparents, parents, and siblings were all very important to him, so many of his poems were about family members. And he developed his distinctive style of writing quickly. His early rhymes were the kind of poems that eventually made him famous.

Even though Ogden was talented at composing humorous rhymes, he preferred writing more serious poetry. He attended high school at St. George's School in Newport, Rhode Island. There Ogden began to write poetry for family members, friends, the school paper, and the local newspaper.

After he graduated from St. George's School in 1920, Nash went to Harvard University in Cambridge, Massachusetts. However, his college career was cut short. After just one year, Nash left Harvard to support himself and help his family.

Over the next few years, Nash worked instead of attending college. For the first time, he lived on his own and not with his parents. He also moved from state to state as he changed jobs.

Nash first returned to Rhode Island. He became a schoolteacher at his old high school, St. George's, where he taught French. Although he enjoyed life as a teacher, Nash left St. George's after one year. He wanted to try his luck in New York City.

Not only was New York a new place for Nash to live, it gave him the opportunity to try a new career as well. He became a bond salesman on Wall Street. A bond is a guarantee issued by the government. The guarantee states that a certain amount of money will be paid to the person who holds the bond on a specific date in the future. Unfortunately, however, even after working as a bond salesman for about a year and a half, Nash sold just one bond—to his godmother!

When selling bonds did not work out, Nash found a new position in the copy department of Barron Collier, an advertising agency. In this job, Nash wrote advertisements that were displayed on streetcars. This type of work was quite similar to his earlier attempts at writing poems—both required imagination and creativity.

During this period, Nash met Joseph Alger. Nash and Alger became quite close friends and even co-authored a children's book. It was titled *The Cricket of Carador.* At the young age of twenty-three, Nash became a published author! Although the book was not very successful, Nash enjoyed writing it and learned a great deal from the experience.

Nash's next job began in 1925, when he joined the publisher Doubleday, Page and Company, working in the editorial and publicity departments. Nash enjoyed this job for a number of reasons. For one thing, he was able to work with successful writers of the time.

It was also at Doubleday that Nash began to write poems again. On days when he had free time at the office, he would write amusing rhymes. His boss and mentor, Dan Longwell, thought Nash's poems were very funny. Longwell encouraged Nash to send these poems to the *New Yorker* magazine. To Nash's surprise, the selective magazine accepted the poems and published them.

After a few of his poems were published in the *New Yorker*, Nash began to gather together the many poems he had written over the years. He compiled these poems, wrote new ones, and organized the whole group to form his first book of poems, titled *Hard Lines*. This book, published in 1931, was a huge success. It was printed seven times in that single year and sold out each time! Nash's career as a writer of humorous poetry, also called light verse, took off quickly.

Also in 1931, Nash married Frances Leonard and moved to Baltimore, Maryland, where he became a freelance writer and worked from home. The Nashes had two daughters, Linell and Isabel.

Nash's daughter Linell describes how her father worked: "My father's work was all over the house. While his official workplace was either the library or the upstairs sitting room, his yellow legal pads would often find their way to the living-room coffee table. His notes to himself would be on scratch pads by telephones or on market lists or old envelopes. He always gathered these things up, and sometimes years later, when its time was ripe, one of these ideas or funny rhymes would suddenly appear in print."

As Nash worked at being a full-time writer, he realized that publishers were more impressed with his humorous poems than with his serious ones. Thus, he focused primarily on writing light verse. This wasn't hard for Nash, because he saw humor in ordinary things and situations. The titles of his poems, which include "The Parsnip," "The Germ," and "The Common Cold," reflect his lighthearted point of view.

Although people often assume that writing playful poems and rhymes was easy for Nash, he actually found it difficult. He would think of an unusual-sounding word, then struggle to rhyme it with another word. His friends and family reported that it was typical for him to jot down a word he wanted to rhyme on a scrap of paper, think of a word that rhymed with it a month or two later, and put the two words into a poem some years after that!

As Nash's career developed, he was able to devote more time to composing the serious poetry that he found most rewarding. When he wasn't writing poetry, he wrote children's books, scripts for movies and plays, and songs for musicals and television shows. One of his most popular children's books is *Custard the Dragon*, a story about a cowardly dragon who belongs to a little girl.

Nash also frequently gave lectures and readings across the United States and England. He spoke on radio shows and appeared on television panels. Often he traveled for two or three months at a time. During these travels, he wrote daily letters, postcards, and poems to his wife and daughters. He told them about his experiences, often composing new poems as he did so.

Late in his career, Nash commented, "I made up my mind long ago that I'd rather be a great bad poet than a bad good poet. . . . As a small boy, I wanted to be a serious poet, . . . but my serious poems were very, very bad. My humorous verses are really a mocking of those attempts. I thought I'd better laugh at myself before everyone laughed at me."

Although people chuckled at his humorous rhymes, they did not laugh at Ogden Nash. They respected the man and his work. In fact, he has been called "America's most popular and frequently quoted contemporary poet."

Ogden Nash died in 1971 after a forty-year career in which he wrote nineteen books of poetry for children and adults.

Turn the page to find a list of some of these books.

Works by Ogden Nash

Here is a partial list of Ogden Nash's books, including poetry.

The Cricket of Carador (1925)

Family Reunion (1950)

Parents Keep Out: Elderly Poems for Youngerly Readers (1951)

The Christmas That Almost Wasn't (1957)

Custard the Dragon (1959; also published as *The Tale of Custard the Dragon*)

Beastly Poetry (1960)

Custard the Dragon and the Wicked Knight (1961)

The New Nutcracker Suite, and Other Innocent Verses (1962)

Everyone but Thee and Me (1962)

A Boy and His Room (1963)

The Adventures of Isabel (1963)

The Untold Adventures of Santa Claus (1964)

The Animal Garden (1965)

The Cruise of the Aardvark (1967)

There's Always Another Windmill (1968)